# The Knife Markets
# OF SANAA

**Rob Waring,** *Series Editor*

**HEINLE**
CENGAGE Learning™

Australia • Brazil • Japan • Korea • Mexico • Singapore • Spain • United Kingdom • United States

# Words to Know

This story is set in a country in the Middle East called Yemen [yɛmən]. It happens in the city of Sanaa [sɑnɑ].

**A** **In the *Souq*.** Read the paragraph. Use the correct form of the underlined words to complete the definitions.

There are *souqs* [suks], or <u>markets</u>, in many countries in the Middle East. *Souqs* are full of small <u>stalls</u> where people can buy <u>spices</u> for food, beautiful <u>jewelry</u>, and special <u>knives</u>. These knives are often heavily <u>decorated</u> and are very expensive. However, the high cost is not only related to money.

**1.** A place where people go to buy and sell things is a _____.

**2.** _____ are tools used for cutting.

**3.** Objects that people wear to look more attractive are _____.

**4.** _____ are plant-based products that add flavor to food.

**5.** A small shop with an open front in a public place is a _____.

**6.** _____ means that something has been added to an item to make it more attractive.

knives

food spices

gold jewelry

**The *Souq***

**B** **The *Jambiya*.** Read the paragraph, then look at the pictures. Write the correct item number next to each **bolded** word.

The *jambiya* [dʒæmbi̯ə] is very important to the men of Yemen. This special knife has a hooked, or rounded, **blade** (   ). The men of Yemen usually wear a *jambiya* in their **belt** (   ). The **handle** (   ) of the *jambiya* is often made from a **rhinoceros' horn** (   ). It can also be made from **water buffalo horns** (   ), or **camel hooves** (   ).

**A *Jambiya* in a Man's Belt**

It is the beginning of the day in the ancient city of Sanaa, Yemen. The morning **call to prayer**[1] wakes the people who live in this beautiful city. This call to prayer has been the same for hundreds of years here.

Sanaa, Yemen's capital city, is in one of the higher areas of Yemen. It has many mountains and hills around it. It's a very special place in many ways. This beautiful city is one of the oldest cities in the world. People have lived here for thousands of years!

---

[1]**call to prayer:** a sound that tells Muslim people that it's time to show respect to their god

🎧 CD 1, Track 09

In the more ancient parts of the city, there are several very tall houses. These houses are made from **mud**[2] and are very close together. They're also covered with white **plaster**.[3] To some, this combination makes Sanaa look like a city that is made of **gingerbread**.[4]

---

[2]**mud:** a soft combination of water and earth
[3]**plaster:** a white material that is put on walls of buildings
[4]**gingerbread:** a kind of cake that is decorated with white topping

Some people think that the mud and white plaster houses of Sanaa look like cake!

Sanaa is a place of beauty and tradition. Here, the busy *souqs* of the city are spread out over several streets. In these *souqs*, the people of Yemen, or Yemenis, **bargain**[5] for spices, jewelry, and other products. People have done this traditional activity for hundreds of years.

Throughout the day, people buy and sell a lot of different and interesting items at the stalls in these markets. However, there is one thing here that is very special to the people of Yemen. Any visitor who walks through the streets of the *souq* will quickly notice it: the *jambiya*.

---

[5]**bargain:** when a buyer and seller work together to agree on a price

The *jambiya* is something that most Yemeni men are hardly ever without. These large, beautifully decorated knives are very important here. Because they are so important, the men of Yemen usually wear the knives in a special thick belt. They want everyone to be able to see their *jambiya*. They want people to see how big, beautiful, or specially decorated their knives are.

The *jambiya*, with its large blade, may look dangerous to some people. However, these days it's almost never used as a **weapon**.[6] It is a **status symbol**[7] and a sign of Yemeni **manhood**.[8]

[6]**weapon:** object used in fighting or war, such as a gun or knife
[7]**status symbol:** something that shows that a person is important
[8]**manhood:** qualities related to being a man and not a boy

In the busy market, **blacksmiths**[9] carefully shape metal into the unusual hooked blades. These very special knives are everywhere in the *souq*. Several of the stalls have rows of the beautiful *jambiya* for people to look at and buy.

---

[9]**blacksmith:** someone whose job is to make things from metal

a row of *jambiya* knives

a blacksmith

metal

Blacksmiths shape metal into jambiya blades.

13

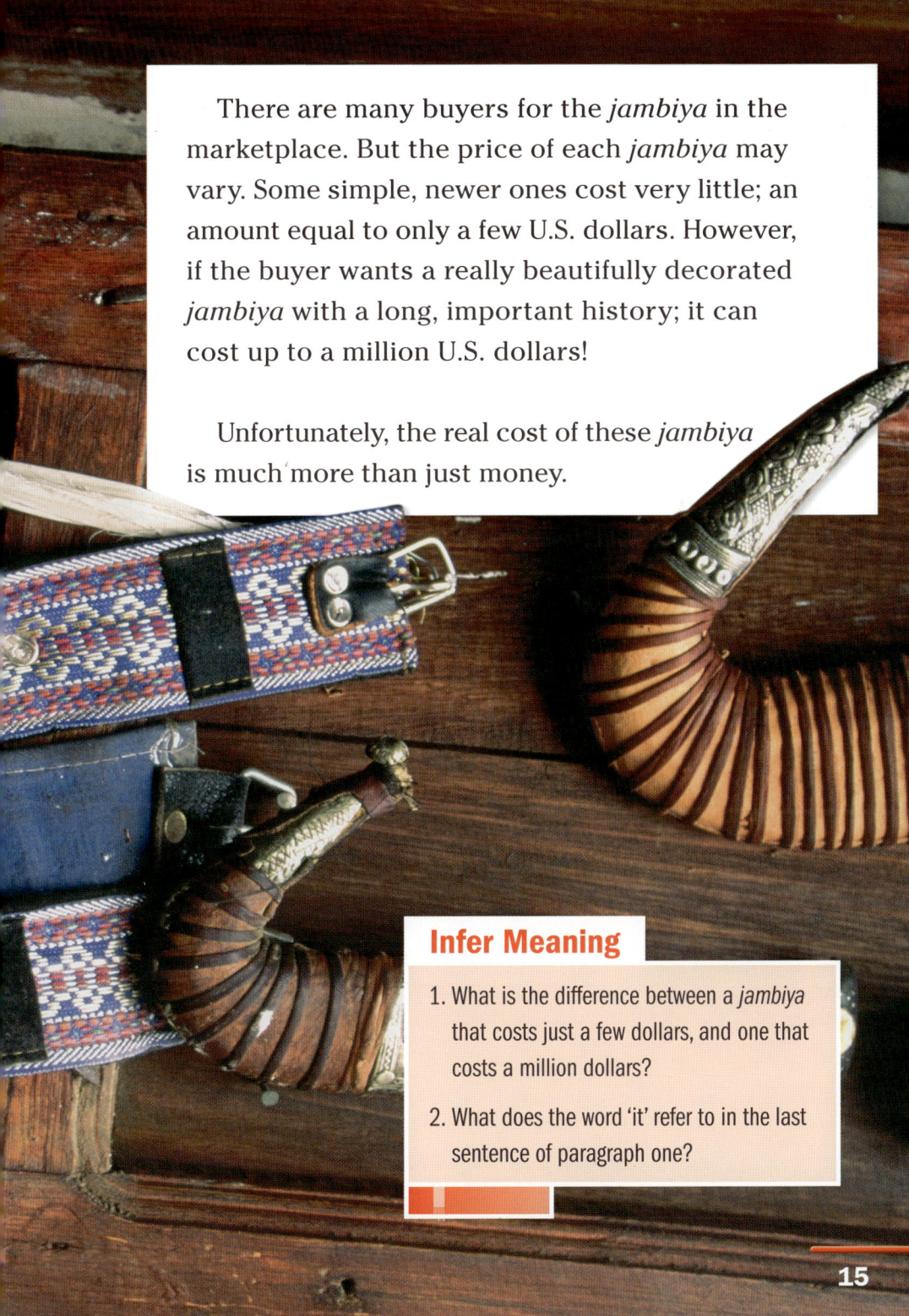

There are many buyers for the *jambiya* in the marketplace. But the price of each *jambiya* may vary. Some simple, newer ones cost very little; an amount equal to only a few U.S. dollars. However, if the buyer wants a really beautifully decorated *jambiya* with a long, important history; it can cost up to a million U.S. dollars!

Unfortunately, the real cost of these *jambiya* is much more than just money.

## Infer Meaning

1. What is the difference between a *jambiya* that costs just a few dollars, and one that costs a million dollars?

2. What does the word 'it' refer to in the last sentence of paragraph one?

The value of these knives often depends on the handle, which is traditionally made from rhinoceros horn. Yemeni knife makers prefer to use rhinoceros horn because it makes the handle very attractive. Because rhinoceros horn is used on *jambiya* handles, many people think the *jambiya* is part of a big problem; the illegal killing of rhinos. These beautiful and unusual animals are in danger. Too many people are killing them to make *jambiya* handles and other things. Soon, there may be none left.

Now, the Yemeni government and international groups are working together. They're trying to stop people from buying and selling rhinoceros horns. However, the tradition of using rhinoceros horn on *jambiya* is very strong. Some knife makers will not stop using this material.

Conservationists[10] and government members are also trying another way to get the knife makers to change. They are encouraging them to use other materials for *jambiya* handles. They want the knife makers to use water buffalo horn or camel hooves for the handles instead. But in Yemen, tradition is very strong, and change is sometimes slow. Unfortunately, a *jambiya* that is made from rhinoceros horn may still be a status symbol here for a long time to come.

---

[10]**conservationist:** someone who works to save or protect the environment

## What do you think?

1. How do you feel about using animals to make products for sale?

2. What other things can the Yemeni government do to stop knife makers from using rhinoceros horn?

# After You Read

1. Which is NOT true about the morning call to prayer?
   A. It happens early.
   B. It happens only in ancient cities.
   C. It happens in Yemen.
   D. It has happened for a long time.

2. In paragraph 2 on page 4, 'it' in 'it has many' refers to:
   A. higher areas
   B. Yemen
   C. Yemen's capital city
   D. tall houses

3. Which is a good heading for page 6?
   A. People of Sanaa Like Gingerbread
   B. Living Inside a Cake House
   C. Mud and Plaster Make Gingerbread
   D. Homes Look Like Decorated Cake

4. Which do people buy in the markets?
   A. spices
   B. traditions
   C. *souqs*
   D. houses

5. In paragraph 2 on page 9, 'throughout' means:
   A. without
   B. in the middle of
   C. during
   D. especially in

6. The *jambiya* is a special traditional knife worn _____ Yemeni men.
   A. in
   B. by
   C. with
   D. of

**7.** For Yemeni men, what is the *jambiya* a symbol of?
   **A.** childhood
   **B.** fighting
   **C.** danger
   **D.** importance

**8.** *Jambiya* are _____ bought in the markets of Sanaa.
   **A.** rarely
   **B.** sometimes
   **C.** often
   **D.** never

**9.** In paragraph 1 on page 16, what does 'illegal' mean?
   **A.** not allowed
   **B.** traditional
   **C.** uncontrolled
   **D.** apparent

**10.** What is the main purpose of page 16?
   **A.** to explain why there is a problem with *jambiya*
   **B.** to show the beauty of the knives in detail
   **C.** to communicate that rhinos are not in danger
   **D.** to teach how the knives are so unusual

**11.** The Yemeni government wants the knives to be made from:
   **A.** rhinoceros horns
   **B.** water buffalo horns
   **C.** camel horns
   **D.** all of the above

**12.** What does the writer think will probably happen to the handles?
   **A.** They will be made from a new material soon.
   **B.** The knife makers will stop making them.
   **C.** The conservationists will make change happen.
   **D.** Nothing will change quickly.

Dear Sarah,

Thanks for your letter. How are you? I have lots of news for you! I have finally arrived in Savannakhet, Laos. I started my new job last week and I've had a lot to do ever since. Right now it's 6:00 in the morning and I've just returned from shopping in the morning market. I know 6:00 is really early, but the market actually opens at 5:00! If you arrive any later than 5:30, all the best food has been sold.

The morning market is really interesting. It's in an old building, however, the building doesn't have a floor. You actually walk through mud inside it! Most of the sellers sit in stalls with their products displayed on the ground in front of them. The market is divided into sections. The food is in one area, the jewelry in another, and clothing in another. Outside of the market, some men sell objects that they have made by hand. However, most of the sellers at the market are women. It's generally the women who make and sell the products.

**Savannakhet is in the south of Laos.**

**Morning Market**

I don't have any way to keep food cold, so shopping has become an everyday activity for me. Bargaining is a big part of shopping in Laos. When I came here, I didn't know anything about this skill. It has not been easy for me to learn. I understood quickly that it's necessary to bargain for everything you buy. If you don't bargain, it's a bad message to people here. It's like saying, "I have lots of money. I don't need to talk about price with you." I enjoy bargaining now as it is a chance to communicate with local people. The morning market allows me to practice my Laotian language skills. They're improving all the time!

I still want to tell you about the evening market, but that will have to wait for another letter!

Your brother,
John

CD 1, Track 10

**Word Count:** 320
**Time:** _____

# Vocabulary List

**bargain** (9)
**belt** (3, 10, 13)
**blacksmith** (12, 13)
**blade** (3, 10, 12)
**call to prayer** (4)
**camel hooves** (3, 19)
**conservationist** (19)
**decorate** (2, 6, 10, 15)
**gingerbread** (6)
**handle** (3, 16, 19)
**jewelry** (2, 9)
**knife** (2, 3, 10, 12, 16, 19)
**manhood** (10)
**market** (2, 9, 15)
**mud** (6, 7)
**plaster** (6, 7)
**rhinoceros horn** (3, 16, 19)
**spice** (2, 9)
**stall** (2, 9, 12)
**status symbol** (10, 19)
**water buffalo horn** (3, 19)
**weapon** (10)